DATE DUE

Dinosaurs and Prehistoric Animals

Pteranodon

by Janet Riehecky

Consulting Editor: Gail Saunders-Smith, PhD

Consultant: Jack Horner, Curator of Paleontology
Museum of the Rockies
Bozeman, Montana

Capstone
press

Mankato, Minnesota

Pebble Plus is published by Capstone Press,
151 Good Counsel Drive, P.O. Box 669, Mankato, Minnesota 56002.
www.capstonepress.com

1 2 3 4 5 6 11 10 09 08 07 06

Library of Congress Cataloging-in-Publication Data
Riehecky, Janet, 1953–
     Pteranodon / by Janet Riehecky.
     p. cm.—(Pebble plus. Dinosaurs and prehistoric animals)
     Summary: "Simple text and illustrations present the life of pteranodon, how it looked, and its behavior"—
Provided by publisher.
     Includes bibliographical references and index.
     ISBN-13: 978-0-7368-5355-2 (hardcover)
     ISBN-10: 0-7368-5355-3 (hardcover)
     1. Pteranodon—Juvenile literature. I. Title. II. Series.
QE862.P7R54 2006
567.918—dc22   2005020865

Editorial Credits
Sarah L. Schuette, editor; Linda Clavel, designer; Wanda Winch, photo researcher

Illustration and Photo Credits
Jon Hughes, illustrator
The Natural History Museum, London, 21

The author dedicates this book to her niece Emylie.

Note to Parents and Teachers

The Dinosaurs and Prehistoric Animals set supports national science standards related
to the evolution of life. This book describes and illustrates pteranodon. The images
support early readers in understanding the text. The repetition of words and phrases
helps early readers learn new words. This book also introduces early readers to subject-
specific vocabulary words, which are defined in the Glossary section. Early readers may
need assistance to read some words and to use the Table of Contents, Glossary, Read
More, Internet Sites, and Index sections of the book.

Table of Contents

pteranodon (terr-AN-oh-don)

A Flying Reptile

Pteranodon was

a prehistoric flying reptile.

Its wings opened

as wide as a small airplane.

Pteranodon lived near
oceans in North America
and Europe.
It lived about
85 million years ago.

How Pteranodon Looked

Pteranodon was as heavy
as a young child.
It weighed about 37 pounds
(17 kilograms).

Pteranodon had
a long crest
on its head.

Pteranodon had
a pointed beak.
It did not have teeth.

Pteranodon had thin legs
and small feet.
Leathery skin
covered its body.

What Pteranodon Did

Pteranodon flew
in the sky for days
without stopping.
It searched for food.

Pteranodon swooped
over the water.
It scooped up fish
and swallowed them whole.

The End of Pteranodon

Pteranodons died about
65 million years ago.
No one knows why
they all died.
You can see pteranodon
fossils in museums.

Glossary

beak—the hard part of a pteranodon's mouth

crest—a flat plate of bone on a pteranodon's head

fossil—the remains or traces of an animal
or a plant

museum—a place where objects of art, history,
or science are shown

prehistoric—very, very old; prehistoric means
belonging to a time before history was
written down.

reptile—a cold-blooded animal with a backbone;
most reptiles lay eggs.

Read More

Ashby, Ruth. *Pteranodon: The Life Story of a Pterosaur*. New York: Abrams, 2005.

Cohen, Daniel. *Pteranodon*. Discovering Dinosaurs. Mankato, Minn.: Bridgestone Books, 2001.

Dahl, Michael. *Winged and Toothless: The Adventures of Pteranodon*. Dinosaur World. Minneapolis: Picture Window Books, 2004.

Internet Sites

FactHound offers a safe, fun way to find Internet sites related to this book. All of the sites on FactHound have been researched by our staff.

Here's how:

1. Visit *www.facthound.com*

2. Type in this special code **0736853553** for age-appropriate sites. Or enter a search word related to this book for a more general search.

3. Click on the **Fetch It** button.

FactHound will fetch the best sites for you!

Index

Word Count: 123
Grade: 1
Early-Intervention Level: 14